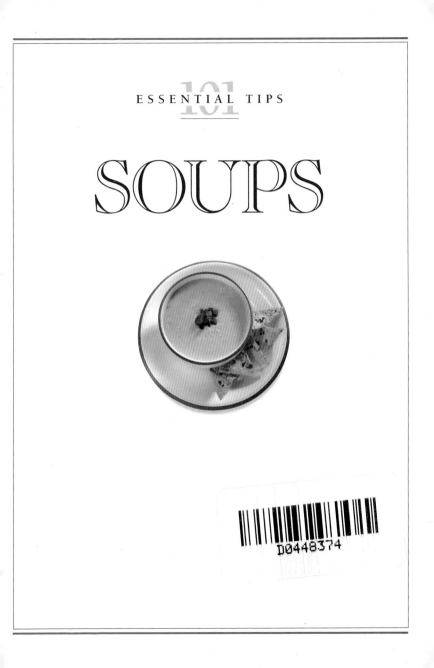

ESSENTIAL TIPS
101

SOUPS

ESSENTIAL TIPS
101

SOUPS

Anne Willan

DK PUBLISHING, INC.

A DK PUBLISHING BOOK

Editor Simon Adams
Art Editor Alison Shackleton
Senior Editor Gillian Roberts
Series Art Editor Alison Donovan
US Editor Laaren Brown

Salt and pepper can be added to most recipes. Season according to your
own taste. Follow either imperial or metric units throughout a recipe,
never a mixture of the two, since they are not exact equivalents.

First American Edition, 1997
2 4 6 8 10 9 7 5 3 1
Published in the United States by DK Publishing, Inc.
95 Madison Avenue, New York, New York 10016

Visit us on the World Wide Web at http://www.dk.com

A catalog record is available from the Library of Congress.
ISBN 0-7894-1980-7

Text film output by The Right Type, Great Britain
Reproduced by Colourscan, Singapore
Printed and bound in Italy by Graphicom

ESSENTIAL TIPS

101

SHORT CUTS

COLD SOUPS

PRESENTATION

SUPER SOUPS

1 A SOUP FOR EVERY OCCASION

A soup can be warmly sustaining in cold weather, or coolly refreshing on a hot day. It can begin a meal as an appertizer before a main course, or balance a light meal of pasta or a sandwich. It can also be a meal in itself, requiring only bread to make it satisfying. Whether hot or cold, a soup can be served on every occasion.

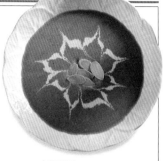

△ SPRING GREEN SOUP

2 MAIN-COURSE SOUPS

Soups such as borscht, chicken and shrimp soup, French onion soup, and chowder can all be served as a main course. For a lighter lunch, serve a creamed or puréed soup, or a cold soup such as Vichyssoise. Accompany these with crackers or a croûton garnish.

◁ CHICKEN & HAM GUMBO

3 SOUPS AS APPETIZERS

Clear soups, such as a light vegetable broth, fruit soups like chilled Hungarian cherry, or a light puréed soup such as red pepper, make ideal appetizers. Choose a hot or cold soup, depending on the menu – and the weather.

LIGHT VEGETABLE BROTH ▷

4 EQUIPMENT NEEDED

Most soups can be made with just a few standard kitchen utensils. A sharp chef's knife and a cutting board are essential for chopping vegetables and other ingredients. You will also need a small knife, a vegetable peeler, a grater, a lemon squeezer, and a selection of wooden spoons. A ladle is also handy.

△ VEGETABLE PEELER

VEGETABLE GRATER ▷

△ WOODEN SPOONS

△ LADLE

△ SHARP KNIVES

▷ SET OF SAUCEPANS

5 SAUCEPANS

Use a large pot or a saucepan with a lid to make hot soups or prepare stocks. Smaller saucepans are required to prepare ingredients. Some hearty soups that require lengthy cooking are best made in a heavy casserole. When using acidic ingredients, do not use aluminum pans as they give a metallic taste.

6 FOOD PROCESSOR OR BLENDER?

FOOD PROCESSOR ▷

Use a food processor to produce a purée with an even, slightly textured consistency. A processor is not suitable for soups containing a lot of starchy vegetables, especially potatoes, since it turns them into a gluey pulp. Use a blender to produce a smoother purée and to thicken any soup slightly. A blender will not break down firm-textured ingredients unless they are thoroughly cooked.

MAKING STOCKS

7 CHICKEN STOCK
Makes about 8 cups (2 liters)

Ingredients
*5lb (2.25kg) free-range
chicken or stewing fowl
2 onions
2 carrots
2 celery ribs
1 bouquet garni
10 black peppercorns
8 cups (2 liters) water*

1 Put the chicken into a large pot.
2 Peel and quarter the onions. Quarter the carrots and celery ribs. Add to the pan with the bouquet garni and peppercorns.
3 Add water just to cover the ingredients. Bring slowly to a boil. Simmer, skimming the surface occasionally with a large metal spoon, for up to 3 hours. Add more water if necessary to keep ingredients covered. The longer the chicken stock is simmered, the more flavor it will have.

4 Strain the stock through a sieve into a large bowl. Let cool, then chill. When cold, remove solid fat from surface. Store in refrigerator and use as needed.

FREEZING STOCK
To freeze chicken or any other stock, pour measured amounts into microwave-safe containers. Use an ice-cube tray for small portions.

△ STRAIN THE STOCK

8 VEGETABLE STOCK
Makes 6 cups (1.5 liters)

Ingredients
3 onions
3 or 4 carrots
3 celery ribs
2 garlic cloves (optional)
8 cups (2 liters) water
1 bouquet garni
10 black peppercorns

1 Peel, chop, and coarsely dice the onions.
2 Peel and dice carrots.
3 Trim and dice celery (*Tip 13*).
4 If using garlic, set the flat side of chef's knife on top of the garlic clove and strike it firmly with your fist. Discard the skin.
5 Put vegetables into a large saucepan. Add water, bouquet garni, and peppercorns.
6 Bring slowly to a boil. Simmer, uncovered, for 1 hour. Skim stock occasionally with a large metal spoon.
7 Remove from the heat. Strain the stock through a sieve into a bowl. Let cool, then cover and store in the refrigerator.

REFRIGERATING STOCK
You can refrigerate any stock for up to 3 days, although it will lose some of its flavor.

---

9 FISH STOCK
Makes 4 cups (1 liter)

Ingredients
1½ lb (750g) white fish bones and heads
1 onion & 3–5 sprigs parsley or 2 bay leaves
1 cup (250ml) dry white wine, or juice of ½ lemon
4 cups (1 liter) water
5 black peppercorns

1 Thoroughly wash fish bones and heads. Cut bones into 4 or 5 pieces.
2 Peel, trim, and thinly slice onion.
3 Put fish bones and heads into a medium pan with onion slices, parsley sprigs or bay

△ ADD WATER TO PAN

leaves, wine or lemon juice, water, peppercorns.
4 Bring slowly to a boil. Simmer, 20 minutes. Skim surface occasionally. Do not allow to boil or to simmer too long or it will taste bitter.
5 Strain stock through a sieve into a bowl. Let cool, then cover and store in the refrigerator.

SEASONING STOCK
Never add seasoning to a stock when making it; it may be reduced later and the flavors will intensify.

---

10 BEEF STOCK

Makes 8–12 cups (2–3 liters)

Ingredients
4½ lb (2kg) beef bones
2 onions & 2 carrots
2 celery ribs
16 cups (4 liters) water
1 bouquet garni
10 black peppercorns
1 garlic clove
1 tbsp tomato paste

STRONGER STOCK
If the flavor of the stock is not strong enough, boil down to concentrate.

1 Heat oven to 450°F/230°C. Put beef bones into large roasting pan; roast until well browned, turning occasionally, 40 minutes.
2 Peel and quarter onions and carrots. Quarter celery ribs. Add vegetables to pan; roast until brown, stirring occasionally, 15–20 minutes.
3 Transfer bones and vegetables to large saucepan. Discard fat from roasting pan; add 2 cups (500ml) of water. Bring to a boil, stirring to dissolve pan juices.
4 Add liquid to pan with remaining ingredients; add enough water to cover bones. Slowly bring to a boil; lower heat; simmer gently, uncovered, for 4–5 hours. Add more water to cover bones.
5 Strain stock. Let cool, then chill. When cold, remove solid fat from surface.

11 CLARIFYING

Clarifying is the process used to produce a clear soup, such as a consommé, from a stock of cooked ingredients. Prepare the ingredients as directed and bring slowly to a boil, then simmer. As the stock simmers, the egg whites and flavorings will form a layer on the surface. This layer is known as the clarification filter.

1 ◁ With a ladle, make a hole in the filter so that the consommé can simmer without breaking up the filter.

2 ▷ When filter has formed a crust, drain through a lined sieve. Draw a paper towel over surface to remove any fat.

INGREDIENTS & PREPARATION

12 BASIC VEGETABLES

Most soups contain vegetables, including at least one member of the onion family. Use fresh vegetables wherever possible. Peel and wash well to remove any dirt and pesticides.

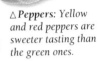

△ *Peppers:* Yellow and red peppers are sweeter tasting than the green ones.

△ *Mushrooms:* Cultivated or wild mushrooms add flavor and texture.

△ *Onions:* Finely diced onions add body to any soup; browned onions add flavor.

△ *Potatoes:* Use diced or puréed potatoes to give soup bulk.

▷ *Carrots:* Tender young carrots have a sweeter flavor.

△ *Tomatoes:* Purée tomatoes and add for a richer color and flavor.

◁ *Leeks:* Wash leeks well to remove any dirt and grit before cooking.

▷ *Celery:* Peel celery to remove tough strings before use.

13 HOW TO DICE VEGETABLES

Sharp knives are essential when dicing vegetables. Grasp the knife firmly with all four fingers wrapped around the handle. Use your free hand to grip the vegetable and guide the blade as you cut.

1 △ Peel or trim vegetable; square off sides if necessary. Cut into ½in (1.25cm) slices.

2 △ Stack the slices and cut downward through them to make ½in (1.25cm) strips.

3 △ Gather the strips into a pile; cut them crosswise to produce even ½in (1.25cm) dice.

△ DICING CELERY
Cut sticks into 3in (7.5cm) pieces, then cut into 2–3 strips. Stack; cut into dice.

△ CHOPPING CABBAGE
Trim outer leaves; cut into quarters. Lay flat on board and cut into fine shreds.

△ CUTTING GREEN BEANS
Trim off ends of beans; cut the beans crosswise into even ½in (1.25cm) pieces.

14 HOW TO DICE CARROTS

Wash carrots, and peel and trim off the ends. Cut each carrot into 3in (7.5cm) pieces. Cut each piece lengthwise into quarters to make sticks; for thicker carrots, you might need to cut more sticks. Gather the sticks together and cut across them to make medium dice. If you cut the dice too small, they may disintegrate during cooking.

15 HOW TO CUT JULIENNE STRIPS

Vegetables cut into julienne strips the size of fine matchsticks are easy to prepare and quick to cook. Use a sharp chef's knife and make sure you hold the vegetable securely while cutting it.

1 △ Peel and trim the vegetable, then cut it into pieces 2–3in (5–7.5cm) long.

2 △ With rounded vegetables, cut a strip from one side so that it lies flat on the board.

3 △ Cut lengthwise into thin slices. Stack; keep knife tip on board and cut into fine strips.

16 CHOPPING ONIONS OR SHALLOTS

The size of the dice when chopping onions or shallots depends on the size of the slice. For a standard size, make slices ¼in (5mm) thick. For finely diced onions or shallots, slice thinner.

1 △ Place onion or shallot on a cutting board. Hold firmly with one hand and cut it lengthwise in half.

2 △ Lay each half, cut side down, on the board. Slice horizontally to the root, leaving the slices attached at the root.

3 △ Slice vertically, again leaving the root end uncut. Finally, cut across all slices to make neat dice.

17 CHOPPING IN A FOOD PROCESSOR

To save time, chop vegetables in a food processor. Wash all vegetables thoroughly, especially leeks, since dirt and grit collect in their leaves. Prepare and trim all vegetables and cut into small chunks. Add to the processor and work until roughly chopped. If you are using tomatoes, add these later and continue to cut until they too are chopped. The longer you run the machine, the finer the pieces will be.

18 STORING CUT VEGETABLES

Vegetables such as potatoes, turnips, parsnips, and green cabbage will quickly discolor after trimming, peeling, and cutting. If you are not using these vegetables immediately, put the pieces in a bowl of cold water so that they do not darken before cooking. When you are ready to use them, drain the water and dry the vegetables thoroughly with a dish towel or paper towels.

19 HOW TO PREPARE PEPPERS

Peppers are mild members of the capsicum family, which also includes hot peppers. Their cores and seeds must be removed and discarded before serving. Cut around each pepper core with a chef's knife to release the core, and pull it out. Then halve each pepper lengthwise. Slice or dice the cored pepper; serve raw or cooked.

1 △ Scrape out the seeds with a sharp knife and cut away the white ribs on the inside of the pepper.

2 △ Set each pepper half, cut side down, on a work surface. Press it down with your hand to make it easier to slice.

3 △ With a chef's knife, slice each pepper half into strips. To make dice, gather the strips together and cut them across.

20 HOW TO PREPARE MUSHROOMS

Wipe the mushrooms free of dirt and grit with damp paper towels. If necessary, rinse them quickly in water for a few seconds. Do not soak since they will quickly become waterlogged and mushy.

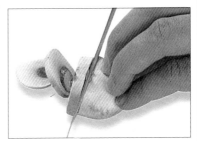

1 △ With a small knife, trim the mushroom stems just level with the caps. If using wild mushrooms, trim just the end of the stems.

2 △ To slice, hold the mushrooms stem side down on the cutting board. Cut them vertically with a knife into slices of the required thickness.

21 HOW TO PEEL & CHOP GARLIC

The strength of garlic varies with its age and dryness. Use more when the garlic is very fresh. To prepare garlic for use, break up the bulb into individual cloves. Then follow the instructions below.

1 △ To loosen the skin, lightly crush each garlic clove by pressing your hand down on the flat side of a chef's knife.

2 △ Peel the skin from the clove with your fingers. Set the flat side of the chef's knife on top and strike with your fist.

3 △ Finely chop the garlic clove with the chef's knife, pivoting the blade back and forth to dice the garlic finely.

22 HOW TO SLICE & WASH LEEKS

Leeks are often gritty, so they need careful preparation before cooking. Prepare and wash them as shown here to ensure that the grit will be left in the water. Drain the leeks in a colander.

1 △ Trim the leeks and discard the roots and tough green tops.

2 △ Using a chef's knife, slit the leeks lengthwise in half.

3 △ Cut crosswise into thin slices. Wash in cold water; drain well.

23 HOW TO PEEL A TOMATO

You may want to peel and seed tomatoes before chopping them. Once the skin is peeled off with a chef's knife, cut each tomato crosswise in half, squeeze out the seeds, and coarsely chop.

1 ◁ Cut out the core and score an X on the base with the tip of a small knife.

2 ▷ Drop into boiling water until the skin splits. Transfer to cold water; peel off the skin.

24 HOW TO PEEL CELERY

Celery can be very stringy and should be peeled. First trim the celery ribs of any leaves and roots. Then peel the strings from the sides of each rib with a knife or a vegetable peeler. The celery is now ready to be cut into strips and diced for cooking, if required.

25 HERBS

Aromatic fresh herbs, such as parsley, mint, basil, tarragon, and cilantro, can transform even the most mundane of soup ingredients. Don't be afraid to experiment.

△ BAY LEAF

△ TARRAGON

PARSLEY ▷

△ BASIL

◁ MINT

△ CILANTRO

FLAT-LEAF PARSLEY ▷

◁ THYME

26 HOW TO CHOP HERBS

To chop herbs, use a sharp knife. Hold the tip of the blade against the cutting board and pivot the knife back and forth until all the leaves or stalks are finely chopped.

Gather up chive stalks before chopping

△ MORE FLAVOR
Chopping herbs releases their essential oils, which will flavor other ingredients.

27 HOW TO MAKE A BOUQUET GARNI

To make a bouquet garni, hold together 2–3 sprigs of fresh thyme, 1 bay leaf, and 5–6 parsley stalks. Wind a piece of white string around the stalks and tie securely.

SAFE STRING ▽
Always use white, untreated string when making a bouquet garni.

Parsley

Bay

Thyme

28 SPICES

Spices can accent the underlying character of a soup, and transform even basic ingredients into something special. The availability of Asian ingredients such as fresh ginger increases the choice considerably. Use spices sparingly at first if unfamiliar with them.

△ DRIED CHILIES

△ FRESH CHILIES

◁ CLOVES

FRESH GINGER ▷

△ CAYENNE PEPPER

△ JUNIPER BERRIES

△ BLACK PEPPERCORNS

△ CINNAMON STICKS

29 HOW TO PREPARE GINGER

Fresh ginger is peeled like a vegetable or a thin-skinned fruit, then sliced and chopped. It is important to chop the root finely, so that the flavor will spread evenly throughout the dish.

1 △ Peel the ginger. Slice through center lengthwise, cutting almost in half.

2 △ Open ginger out; place flat side down. Place flat side of knife on ginger; press to crush.

3 △ Holding the pieces together, chop as finely as possible, cutting across the fibrous grain.

CREAMED & PURÉED SOUPS

30 BUTTERNUT SQUASH SOUP

Serves 6

Ingredients

1 onion & 1 garlic clove
1in (2.5cm) ginger
2–3 butternut squash,
about 3lb (1.4kg)
2–3 tart apples
Juice of ½ lemon
3 tbsp butter
4 cups (1 liter) chicken
stock
4 tbsp apple juice

1 Peel and dice onion, garlic, and piece of fresh ginger (*Tip 29*).
2 Peel butternut squash; cut into large pieces.
3 Peel, core, and dice apples.
4 Put apple cubes in a bowl and sprinkle lemon juice over them; toss so they are evenly coated.
5 Melt butter in large pan; add onion, garlic, and ginger. Cook, stirring, until onion is soft, 2–3 minutes. Stir in cubes of butternut squash and apple. Season to taste.
6 Pour in stock; bring to a boil. Cover and simmer gently, stirring occasionally, for about 40 minutes.
7 Remove soup from heat, let cool slightly; purée in a blender.
8 Reheat soup; add apple juice and stir to mix. If the soup is too thick, add a little more stock. Season to taste.

◁ **TO SERVE**
Ladle soup into individual warmed bowls. Garnish with croûtons (Tip 96).

31 HOW TO PREPARE SUMMER SQUASH

Summer squash are members of the gourd family, along with winter squash and pumpkins. Unlike their relatives, summer squash have soft skins that are easily removed with a vegetable peeler. If you use a knife, you will remove too much of the flesh.

1 △ Using a vegetable peeler, remove the skin, working your way toward the bulbous end.

2 △ Cut the squash lengthwise in half and then into quarters. Discard seeds and fibers.

3 △ With a chef's knife, cut the flesh of the squash crosswise into ¾in (2cm) chunks.

32 HOW TO CUT & CORE AN APPLE

You need to work quickly when cutting and coring an apple; the flesh discolors quickly. To prevent this from occurring, sprinkle lemon juice over the cut apple so that it is evenly coated.

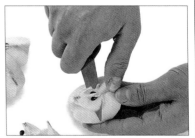

1 △ Peel the skin off each apple with a vegetable peeler. With a small knife, cut the flower and stem ends from each apple. Remove as little flesh as possible.

2 △ Cut each apple in half and then in quarters. Cut out the cores and cut each quarter into ¾in (2cm) cubes. Work quickly before apples discolor.

CREAMED & PURÉED SOUPS

33 PUMPKIN & APPLE SOUP

Serves 6

Bagel chips
are a crisp
contrast

◁ **To Serve**
*Serve with a garnish of
peeled pumpkin seeds
coated in oil and
toasted in a hot oven.*

Ingredients
1 onion & 1 garlic clove
1in (2.5cm) ginger
4lb (1.8kg) pumpkin
2–3 tart apples
Juice of ½ lemon
3 tbsp butter
1 tbsp curry powder
*4 cups (1 liter) chicken
stock & 4 tbsp apple juice*

1 Peel and dice onion, garlic, and piece of fresh ginger (*Tip 29*).
2 Cut out flesh from pumpkin, discarding seeds and fibers. Cut flesh into ¾in (2cm) chunks.
3 Peel, core, and dice apples. Brush with juice.
4 Melt butter in large pot; add onion, garlic, ginger, and curry powder. Cook 2–3 minutes. Stir in pumpkin and apple. Season.
5 Pour in stock; bring to a boil. Cover; simmer gently, stirring occasionally, for 40 minutes.
6 Remove soup from heat and let cool slightly; purée in a blender.
7 Reheat soup; add apple juice and stir to mix. If the soup is too thick, add more stock. Season.

34 SPICED CARROT & ORANGE SOUP
Serves 6

Ingredients
1½ lb (750g) carrots
1 onion & 2 oranges
2 tbsp butter
1½ tsp ground coriander
4 cups (1 liter) chicken
stock
¾ cup (175ml) light cream

TO SERVE ▷
Sprinkle each serving with orange julienne strips and serve immediately.

Use hand blender to purée soup in pan

1 △ Peel, slice carrots; peel, dice onion. Grate zest from 1 orange; peel zest from other; squeeze juice from both to make ½ cup (125ml). Melt butter in pan. Add onion, cook 2–3 minutes. Add carrots, grated zest, coriander. Stir.

2 ▷ Cover pan, cook gently, 10 minutes. Add chicken stock, bring to a boil; simmer 30–40 minutes. Let cool slightly, then purée.

3 △ Reheat soup, then stir in orange juice and ½ cup (125ml) cream. If soup is too thick, stir in more stock. Taste for seasoning; add more coriander and seasoning if required. Use rest of cream to decorate each serving.

4 △ With a chef's knife, cut the pared strips of orange zest into the thinnest possible julienne strips. Drop strips into boiling water. Simmer for 2 minutes. Drain. Rinse with cold water. Drain again. This removes any bitterness from the julienne strips.

35 SPICED CARROT & PARSNIP SOUP

Serves 6

1 Peel and dice 1 onion.
2 Prepare 8 medium carrots and 4 medium parsnips; reserve half a carrot and half a parsnip to make julienne strips. Peel and thinly slice remaining carrots and parsnips.
3 Melt 1 tbsp butter in pot. Add onion, cook 2–3 minutes.
4 Add carrots, parsnips, and 1½ tsp ground cumin. Cover pot, cook gently for 10 minutes.
5 Add 4 cups (1 liter) chicken stock; bring to a boil. Simmer 30–40 minutes.
6 Let cool slightly; purée in pot.
7 Reheat soup, stir in ½ cup (125ml) light cream.

△ TO SERVE
Deep-fry reserved vegetable strips until brown, 30–60 seconds. Use as garnish.

36 CURRIED ZUCCHINI SOUP
Serves 6

Ingredients
1 onion
1 garlic clove
2lb (1kg) zucchinis
2 medium potatoes
3 tbsp butter
2 tbsp curry powder
4 cups (1 liter) chicken stock

1 Dice the onion and finely chop the garlic (*Tip 21*).

2 Trim zucchinis and halve lengthwise; cut into ½in (1.25cm) slices. Peel and dice potatoes.

3 Melt butter in a large pan. Add onion and garlic with curry powder. Cook gently, stirring well, for 5 minutes.

4 Add stock and potatoes to the pan. Season to taste, then simmer, uncovered, for 15 minutes. Add zucchinis and simmer for 15–20 minutes longer. Do not allow the soup to boil.

5 Remove the soup from the heat, let cool slightly, then purée it with a hand blender. Alternatively, purée the soup in batches in a standard blender or food processor and combine the batches in the pan.

6 Reheat the soup; if too thick, add more stock. Season to taste and serve at once.

◁ **TO SERVE**
Ladle the soup into warmed soup plates and serve with fried herb croûtons (Tip 95) sprinkled on top.

37 CURRY SPICE BLENDS

Commercially prepared ground blends (often labeled mild, medium, or hot) usually mix bay, cumin, coriander, black pepper, turmeric, cinnamon, cardamom, chili, cloves, and salt in varying proportions. Taste the finished dish before adding extra seasoning. If you have made it too hot, serve it with some plain yogurt alongside.

38 PROVENÇAL VEGETABLE SOUP

Serves 6

Ingredients
1 eggplant, about 12oz (375g)
2 large zucchinis
1 large red pepper
2 tbsp olive oil
4 medium plum tomatoes
4 large shallots
4 garlic cloves
2 sprigs fresh oregano
5 sprigs fresh basil
Juice of ½ lemon
4 cups (1 liter) chicken stock

1 Trim and cut eggplant lengthwise in half. Score flesh in a lattice, cutting almost to skin. Sprinkle generously with salt and let stand for 30 minutes to draw out bitter juices.

2 Trim and cut zucchinis lengthwise in half.

3 Core, halve, and seed pepper. Preheat oven to 350°F/180°C.

4 Rinse zucchinis. Place vegetables cut side down in oiled roasting pan. Brush vegetables with olive oil; season. Bake in oven, 25 minutes.

5 Add tomatoes, shallots, and garlic to pan; roast until soft, about 25 minutes more.

6 Strip leaves from oregano and basil, saving some basil leaves for the garnish. Tear leaves.

7 When vegetables are cool, remove flesh and pulp from skins. Cut into chunks; purée until smooth. Transfer to saucepan.

8 Stir in lemon juice, chicken stock, oregano, and basil. Bring to boil; simmer for 10 minutes.

◁ **TO SERVE**
Serve with sesame-seed twists (Tip 98) and garnish with basil leaves.

39 GREEN PEA SOUP WITH MINT
Serves 4–6

Ingredients
1½ lb (750g) fresh peas
1 small round lettuce
6 shallots
6 sprigs fresh mint
2 tbsp butter
3 cups (750ml) vegetable stock
1 tsp sugar
Juice of 1 lemon
½ cup (125ml) heavy cream

TO SERVE ▽
Decorate with cream (Tip 90), shredded lettuce, and mint.

1 Shell peas into large bowl.
2 Pull lettuce leaves from core; wash and dry. Set aside 3 leaves. Tightly roll rest of leaves and cut crosswise into coarse shreds.
3 Peel shallots and dice finely (*Tip 16*).
4 Strip mint leaves off stalks; set aside 6 leaves.
5 Melt butter in saucepan. Add shallots; sauté, stirring until soft but not brown, 2–3 minutes.
6 Add peas; stir in stock, sugar, and seasoning. Bring to boil, cover, and simmer until peas are almost tender, 12–20 minutes.
7 Add shredded lettuce and whole mint leaves. Cover pan; simmer until tender, 5 minutes.
8 Purée soup in blender until smooth. Return to pan. Stir in lemon juice and three-quarters of cream. Bring just to a boil; season.

Parmesan crackers (Tip 99) make an ideal accompaniment

GETTING AHEAD
Fresh green pea soup can be made up to 1 day ahead. Keep it covered in the refrigerator. Just before serving, reheat, and add the garnish.

40 GREEN PEA SOUP WITH TARRAGON
Serves 4–6

Ingredients
1½ lb (750g) fresh peas
6 shallots
1 small round lettuce
4 sprigs fresh tarragon
2 tbsp butter
3 cups (750ml) chicken
stock
1 tsp sugar
4 tbsp heavy cream
Juice of 1 lemon

1 Shell the peas into a bowl.
2 Peel shallots; separate into sections and dice finely (*Tip 16*).
3 Pull lettuce leaves from core; wash and dry. Tightly roll leaves and cut crosswise into coarse shreds.
4 Strip the tarragon leaves from their stalks.
5 Melt butter in saucepan. Add shallots; sauté, stirring until soft but not brown, 2–3 minutes.
6 Add peas; stir in stock, sugar, and seasoning. Bring to boil, cover, and simmer until peas are almost tender, 12–20 minutes.
7 Add lettuce and tarragon leaves. Cover saucepan; simmer until tender, 5 minutes. Remove a few peas for garnish.
8 Purée soup in a blender until smooth. Return to pan, and stir in cream and lemon juice. Bring just to a boil; season to taste.

◁ **TO SERVE**
Serve hot, garnished with reserved peas and accompanied by Parmesan crackers.

41 HOW TO SERVE PEA SOUP COLD
When served cold, this fresh-tasting soup is ideal for a warm summer's day. To serve it cold, make the soup as directed, and then pour it into a large tureen. Cover the tureen, and place it in the refrigerator for at least 3 hours. Garnish before serving.

42 RED PEPPER SOUP WITH PESTO
Serves 6

Ingredients
2 large red peppers
8 medium plum tomatoes
4 shallots
2 garlic cloves
2 tbsp olive oil
4 cups (1 liter)
vegetable stock
2 tsp sugar
Juice of ½ lemon

TO SERVE ▷
Serve the soup from a warmed
tureen. Add a generous portion
of pesto (Tip 44) to each serving.

2 ▽ Add peppers
and tomatoes;
stir in stock and
sugar. Bring to a
boil. Simmer for
15–20 minutes.

1 △ Roast and peel
peppers (Tip 43);
dice. Prepare tomatoes
(Tip 23), shallots (Tip 16).
Chop garlic. Heat oil in a
large saucepan; add garlic,
shallots; sauté 1–2 minutes.

Simmer until
vegetables are
very soft; stir
occasionally

3 △ Remove the soup from the heat and let it cool slightly. Purée in a food processor: the finished consistency should be smooth but not too thick. You may have to purée the soup in 2-3 batches. Return the soup to the pan.

4 △ Add lemon juice and stir well to combine. Warm the soup over low heat, stirring occasionally. Taste, and add more lemon juice, sugar, and seasoning, if required.

43 HOW TO ROAST PEPPERS

Roasting peppers makes them easy to peel and adds a smoky flavor. Heat the grill; set the whole pepper on a rack 4in (10cm) from the heat.

1 △ Grill the pepper for about 10–12 minutes, turning it as necessary, until the skin blackens and blisters. Put the pepper in a heavy plastic bag, close it, and let the pepper cool.

2 △ With your fingers, peel off the skin. Cut around the core and pull it out. Cut the pepper lengthwise in half and scrape out the seeds. Cut away the white ribs on the inside.

44 HOW TO MAKE PESTO

Makes 6 servings

Cilantro pesto
1 bunch fresh cilantro,
    about 1oz (30g)
1 bunch parsley,
    about 1oz (30g)
1 garlic clove
½ cup (60g) pine kernels
½ cup (60g) freshly grated
    Parmesan cheese
4 tbsp olive oil

Basil pesto
2 bunches fresh basil,
    about 1½ oz (45g)
1 garlic clove
½ cup (60g) pine kernels
½ cup (60g) freshly grated
    Parmesan cheese
4 tbsp olive oil

Parmesan cheese

Cilantro

Garlic

Pine kernels

Parsley

1 △ Strip the leaves from the cilantro and parsley stalks. If you are making basil pesto, strip the leaves from the basil stalks. Set the flat side of the chef's knife on the garlic clove and strike it firmly with your fist. Remove and discard the garlic skin.

2 △ Put pine kernels, garlic, Parmesan cheese, herb leaves, and seasoning in a blender or food processor and purée until almost smooth.

3 △ With the blade still turning, gradually add the oil. Scrape down the side of the mixing bowl from time to time with a rubber spatula.

4 △ Taste the pesto for seasoning. If it is very thick, work in a little more oil. Transfer to a bowl; cover and chill until ready to use.

CREAMED & PURÉED SOUPS

45 GOLDEN PEPPER SOUP WITH PESTO
Serves 6

Ingredients
*4 large yellow peppers,
about 2lb (1kg)*
4 shallots
2 garlic cloves
2 tbsp olive oil
*4 cups (1 liter) vegetable
stock*
2 tsp sugar
Juice of 1 lemon

1 Roast, peel, and seed peppers
(*Tip 43*), then dice.
2 Prepare shallots (*Tip 16*);
peel and chop garlic.
3 Heat oil in a large saucepan, add shallots and
garlic, and sauté, stirring, until soft but not
browned, 1–2 minutes.
4 Add the pepper dice to the saucepan, then stir
in vegetable stock and sugar. Bring to a boil.
Simmer the soup, stirring occasionally, until the
vegetables are very soft, 15–20 minutes.
5 Remove the soup from the heat and let it cool
slightly. Purée in a food processor; the finished
consistency should be smooth but not too thick.
Return the soup to the pan.
6 Add lemon juice and stir well to combine.
Warm the soup over low heat, stirring
occasionally. Taste; add more lemon juice,
sugar, and seasoning, if required.

◁ **TO SERVE**
*Drizzle on some basil pesto (Tip 44)
and garnish with a sprig of basil.
Serve rest of pesto in a bowl.*

COLOR CONTRAST
*Intensely colored soups, such as
red or golden pepper soup, look best
when served in white soup bowls.*

33

46 SPRING GREEN SOUP

Serves 6

Ingredients

1 large bunch spinach
1 bunch watercress
1 bunch arugula
2 shallots
3 tbsp butter
¼ cup (30g) all-purpose flour
6 cups (1.5 liters) chicken stock
Pinch of ground nutmeg
½ cup (125ml) heavy cream
Juice of ½ lemon

TO SERVE ▷
Ladle soup into bowls and decorate with cream (Tip 90). Sprinkle with toasted almonds.

Greens will purée easily if you add a little chicken stock

1 △ Discard stalks from spinach, watercress, and arugula. Wash leaves thoroughly. Fill large pan with salted water, bring to a boil, and add greens; simmer until tender, 1–2 minutes. Drain greens in colander; rinse immediately in cold water. Drain well.

2 △ When greens are cool enough to handle, squeeze them to remove excess water. Place in blender; purée well until finely chopped.

3 △ Chop shallots (*Tip 16*). Melt butter in saucepan, add shallots, sauté until soft, 2–3 minutes. Stir in flour and cook for 1–2 minutes. Add stock; bring to a boil. Add nutmeg and seasoning. Simmer 2 minutes.

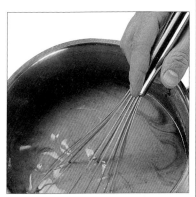

4 △ Add puréed greens to pan and bring almost back to a boil, beating vigorously. Beat in heavy cream; bring just back to a boil. Remove from heat. Add lemon juice and taste for seasoning, adding more lemon juice and seasoning if required.

47 GREEN SOUP WITH CHORIZO

Serves 6

1 Prepare spinach, watercress, arugula, and shallots as in Tip 46, and make soup as directed.
2 Cut 8oz (250g) chorizo, or other spicy sausage, crosswise into very thin slices.
3 Heat 1 tbsp vegetable oil in a frying pan, add sausage slices; sauté until browned and almost crisp, and much of the fat has been cooked out, 5–7 minutes.
4 Remove sausage slices with a slotted spoon; drain very well on paper towels to remove excess fat.
5 Reheat soup if necessary. Stir 2–3 dashes of Tabasco sauce into soup. Add sausage slices.

△ TO SERVE
Divide between six deep bowls. Make sure each serving contains plenty of sausage.

HEARTY SOUPS

48 BORSCHT
Serves 8–10

Stir in sour cream before serving to add richness

Ingredients
1 green cabbage
2 carrots & 3 onions
3–4 sprigs parsley & dill
1½ lb (750g) tomatoes
6 beets, about 2lb (1kg)
4 tbsp butter
8 cups (2 liters)
chicken stock
1 tsp sugar
Juice of 1 lemon
2–3 tbsp red wine
vinegar
½ cup (125ml) sour cream

Piroshki are stuffed with vegetable and cheese mixture

◁ **TO SERVE**
Piroshki (Tip 101) make a substantial accompaniment.

1 ▷ Prepare, slice cabbage, carrots, and onions. Chop herbs (*Tip 26*); prepare tomatoes (*Tip 23*) and beets (*Tip 49*). Melt butter in large saucepan. Add carrots and diced onions. Cook until soft but not brown, 3–5 minutes. Set aside one quarter of sautéed vegetables for piroshki filling (*Tip 101*).

GET AHEAD
Borscht can be prepared and kept, covered, in the refrigerator for 2–3 days; the flavor improves on standing. It can also be frozen without harming the taste.

2 △ Add sliced cabbage, grated beets, chopped tomatoes, chicken stock, and sugar to saucepan, and bring to a boil. Simmer 45–60 minutes. Taste for seasoning and add more sugar if required. Add more stock if the soup remains too thick.

3 △ Just before serving, reheat the soup if necessary. Stir in the chopped parsley and dill, lemon juice, and red wine vinegar; season to taste. Pour the soup into a large warmed tureen to serve. Top with sour cream.

49 HOW TO PREPARE BEETS

Beets need to be cooked and peeled before they can be used in a soup. Never peel a beet before cooking, because it will bleed its crimson dye onto everything with which it comes in contact.

1 △ Trim and scrub the beets. Bring to a boil in a pot half-filled with salted water. Cook for 30 minutes or until tender when tested with a knife.

2 △ Drain the beets. When cool enough to handle, peel off the skin. If you need to grate the beets for a recipe, use the coarse side of the grater.

HEARTY SOUPS

50 RUSTIC BORSCHT
Serves 8–10

Ingredients
3lb (1.4kg) beef shank
1 small green cabbage
2 carrots
2 onions
3–4 sprigs fresh dill
3–4 sprigs fresh parsley
6 beets, about 2lb (1kg)
4 tbsp butter
1 tsp sugar
3 tbsp red wine vinegar
Juice of 1 lemon

To Serve ▷
Serve with piroshki (Tip 101), *sour cream, and herb garnish.*

1 Place beef in salted water and bring to boil.
2 Simmer beef, skimming occasionally, until tender, 3–4 hours.
3 Trim cabbage, discarding any wilted leaves; cut in half and finely shred. Peel and dice carrots (*Tip 14*) and onions (*Tip 16*).
4 Strip herb leaves from stalks; chop finely.
5 Prepare and cook beets (*Tip 49*).
6 Melt butter in a large saucepan; add carrots and onions; cook until soft, 3–5 minutes.
7 Add cabbage, beets, beef stock, and sugar to pan; bring to boil. Simmer 45–60 minutes.
8 Shred beef from the bone and add to soup. Flavor with herbs, vinegar, and lemon juice.

51 HOW TO PREPARE DRIED BEANS

To prepare dried beans for cooking, put the beans into a bowl. Cover generously with cold water and let soak overnight. Drain the beans in a colander, rinse under running water, and drain again. As an alternative to soaking the beans overnight, put them into a saucepan and cover with water. Bring to a boil and let simmer for 1 hour. Drain the beans, rinse with cold water, and drain again.

△ SOAKING BEANS

52 BEAN & VEGETABLE SOUP

Serves 6–8

Ingredients

1 cup (200g) dried beans
½ lb (250g) slab bacon
1 bouquet garni
12 cups (3 liters) chicken stock
1 bunch leeks
2 small turnips
3 large celery ribs
2 medium potatoes
4 medium carrots
½ head green cabbage
¼ lb (125g) green beans
2 garlic cloves

1 Prepare dried beans (*Tip 51*).
2 Rinse the slab bacon, put in saucepan, and cover with cold water. Bring to a boil, simmer for 10 minutes.
3 Put the beans, pork, and bouquet garni into a large pan; add all but 2 cups (500ml) chicken stock. Boil for 10 minutes. Cover pan and simmer for 1 hour.
4 Prepare leeks (*Tip 22*); dice turnips, celery, potatoes, and carrots. Shred cabbage and cut up beans. Prepare garlic (*Tip 21*). Add all to pan.
5 Add rest of stock; bring back to boil. Simmer until meat is tender, about 1½ hours.
6 Remove and discard bouquet garni; remove pork. Discarding fat, cut meat into small cubes. Replace in pan; season to taste. Serve very hot.

Sun-dried tomato croûtes (Tip 92) add a contemporary touch to this soup

TO SERVE ▷
Serve in individual, warmed soup bowls.

53 GERMAN-STYLE SPLIT PEA SOUP

Serves 6–8

Ingredients

4 medium carrots
2 large onions
1 medium rutabaga
2 medium potatoes
2 celery ribs
8oz (250g) dried yellow
  split peas
3 whole cloves
1 bouquet garni
1 smoked ham hock,
  about 1lb (500g)
4 cups (1 liter) water
2 cups (500ml) beer
8oz (250g) frankfurters
1 medium bunch parsley
1 tsp mustard powder

Pumpernickel bread complements this satisfying soup

△ TO SERVE
Ladle soup into warmed soup plates and sprinkle a little of the reserved parsley on each one.

1 ▷ Prepare carrots, onions, rutabaga, potatoes, and celery. Put split peas into a sieve and rinse well. Mix diced vegetables and peas in flameproof casserole. Tuck cloves into bouquet garni and add with bacon, water, and beer to casserole. Bring to a boil and skim off any scum. Cover; simmer until peas are tender, 2–2¼ hours.

MELLOW WITH AGE
The flavor of German split pea soup will mellow if the soup is made up to 2 days ahead. Once the soup is cooked, cool it, and keep covered in the refrigerator. Just before serving, reheat, and add the frankfurters, mustard, and parsley.

Tuck cloves into string wrapped around bouquet garni

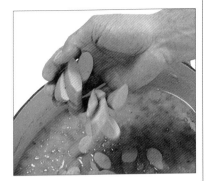

2 △ Cut frankfurters into ½in (1.25cm) slices. Strip parsley leaves from stalks; chop finely. Remove ham hock and bouquet garni from casserole. Cool slightly and pull off meat; chop coarsely. Add meat to soup.

Stir in chopped parsley just before serving so it stays green

3 △ Add frankfurter slices and cook gently until heated, 3–5 minutes. Put mustard powder in small bowl. Spoon in 2 tbsp of soup and stir well. Add mustard mixture and most of chopped parsley to casserole. Season.

54 GREEN SPLIT PEA & BACON SOUP
Serves 6–8

To Serve △
Slices of light rye bread flavored with caraway make a nice accompaniment.

1 Prepare the vegetables as in Tip 53, using green instead of yellow split peas.
2 Mix diced vegetables and peas in flameproof casserole. Add water, bouquet garni, and beer as Tip 53, ½ tsp ground cilantro, and a pinch of ground cloves. Bring to a boil. Cover; simmer until peas are tender, 2–2¼ hours.
3 After about 45 minutes, add 1lb (500g) lean slab bacon.
4 When the split peas are very tender, remove bacon and cut into dice, discarding any rind. Remove and discard bouquet garni.
5 Return bacon to soup; stir in all the chopped parsley. Season well.

55 CHICKEN & HAM GUMBO
Serves 6–8

Ingredients
1 onion & 2 garlic cloves
1 green & 1 red pepper
1 celery rib
1lb (500g) okra
2 medium tomatoes
3 sprigs parsley & thyme
12 chicken thighs
8oz (250g) smoked ham
5 tbsp (75ml) oil
¼ cup (30g) all-purpose flour
2 tbsp tomato paste
4 cups (1 liter) chicken
stock & 1 bay leaf
Pinch of cayenne

1 Prepare and dice onion, garlic, peppers, celery. Trim okra; cut into thin slices. Prepare tomatoes (*Tip 23*).
2 Strip leaves from 3 sprigs each parsley and thyme; coarsely chop leaves.
3 Skin chicken by grasping skin firmly with one hand and pulling it away from meat.
4 Cut ham into ½in (1.25cm) dice.
5 Heat oil in flameproof casserole; stir in flour and cook over low to medium heat, stirring, until flour is a rich brown color, 10–15 minutes.
6 Stir in okra, tomatoes, tomato paste, chicken stock, bay leaf, half of chopped herbs, cayenne. Bring to a boil. Add remaining vegetables and garlic; continue cooking 8–10 minutes.
7 Add chicken thighs; simmer for 30 minutes.
8 Stir in diced ham; simmer until chicken is tender, about 30 minutes.
9 Remove from heat. Take out chicken; pull meat in shreds from bones; stir into gumbo.

◁ **TO SERVE**
Serve on individual plates with rice timbales (Tip 57), and sprinkle with chopped herbs.

56 CHICKEN & SHRIMP SOUP
Serves 4–6

Ingredients
1 onion & 2 garlic cloves
1 small green pepper
1 small red pepper
1 celery rib
2 medium tomatoes
1 medium bunch parsley
2–3 sprigs fresh thyme
6 chicken thighs
1½ lb (750g) large raw shrimp
5 tbsp (75ml) oil
¼ cup (30g) all-purpose flour
2 tbsp tomato paste
4 cups (1 liter) chicken stock
1 bay leaf
Pinch of cayenne
1 tsp ground allspice
Juice of ½ lemon
6 scallions

TO SERVE ▷
Serve with sliced scallions sprinkled on top.

1 Prepare vegetables, herbs, and chicken as in Steps 1–3, Tip 55.
2 Peel and prepare shrimp (*Tip 61*).
3 Heat oil in flameproof casserole; stir in flour and cook over low to medium heat, stirring until flour is a rich brown, 10–15 minutes.
4 Stir in tomatoes, tomato paste, chicken stock, bay leaf, chopped herbs, spices, and lemon juice. Bring to a boil. Add remaining vegetables and garlic; continue cooking until lightly browned, 8–10 minutes.
5 Add chicken thighs; simmer for 45 minutes.
6 Add shrimp; simmer for 15 minutes.
7 Season to taste; serve very hot.

△ RICE WITH SOUP
Rice timbales are an ideal accompaniment to gumbos and other hearty soups.

57 HOW TO MAKE A RICE TIMBALE
Brush a small glass bowl or other similar container with a little oil or melted butter or margarine. Fill with boiled rice; long-grain white rice is best for making a timbale. Press the rice down lightly in the bowl. Turn the bowl upside down onto a warm serving plate and lift off the bowl. A perfectly formed timbale should result every time.

58 NEW ENGLAND FISH CHOWDER
Serves 8

Ingredients
2 medium onions
2 celery ribs
1 medium carrot
3 medium potatoes
6 oz (175g) sliced bacon
2lb (1kg) skinned cod fillets
2lb (1kg) mussels
6 cups (1.5 liters) fish
stock & 2 bay leaves
½ cup (125ml) white wine
2 tsp dried thyme
½ cup (60g) all-purpose
flour
1 cup (250ml) heavy cream

1 Prepare and dice onions, celery, carrot, and potatoes.
2 Cut bacon slices into strips, then dice.
3 Rinse cod fillets in cold water; pat dry with paper towels. Remove any bones; cut fillets into 1in (2.5cm) cubes. Prepare mussels (*Tip 60*).
4 Put fish stock and bay leaves in pan and pour in wine. Heat to boiling; simmer 10 minutes.
5 Put bacon in a flameproof casserole and cook until crisp, 3–5 minutes. Pour off fat.
6 Add vegetables and thyme; cook 5–7 minutes.
7 Sprinkle in flour; cook for 1 minute.
8 Add hot stock mixture and bring to boil. Simmer until tender, 40 minutes.
9 Remove from heat. Mash third of potatoes on casserole side with fork; stir to combine.
10 Return to heat; add mussels. Simmer until shells start to open, 1–2 minutes. Stir in cod; simmer 2–3 minutes.
11 Pour in cream and bring just to a boil.

◁ To Serve
Discard bay leaves and any unopened mussels. Serve hot in bowls; sprinkle with chopped dill.

59 MANHATTAN FISH CHOWDER
Serves 8

Ingredients
2 medium onions
1 carrot & 3 potatoes
2 celery ribs
2½ lb (1.2kg) tomatoes
4 garlic cloves
6oz (175g) sliced bacon
2lb (1kg) skinned cod fillets
2lb (1kg) mussels
6 cups (1.5 liters) fish stock
2 bay leaves
1 cup (250ml) white wine
1 tbsp dried thyme
2 tbsp tomato paste
½ cup (60g) all-purpose flour

1 Prepare and dice
onions, carrot, potatoes, celery, and tomatoes.
2 Prepare and chop garlic (*Tip 21*).
3 Prepare bacon, cod, and mussels as in Tip 58.
4 Cook fish stock, bay leaves, and wine as in
Tip 58. Cook bacon as in Tip 58. Add onions,
carrot, celery, garlic, thyme, and tomato paste;
cook 5–7 minutes.
5 Sprinkle in flour; cook for 1 minute.
6 Add hot stock mixture and bring to boil. Add
potatoes and tomatoes; simmer until vegetables
are tender, about 40 minutes.
7 Add mussels. Simmer until shells start to
open, 1–2 minutes. Stir in cod; simmer 2–3
minutes until fish flakes easily.

*Use large
ladle to serve
chowder in
generous
portions*

◁ **To Serve**
*Sprinkle with
chopped fresh
thyme and serve
with crusty whole-
wheat bread.*

45

60 HOW TO PREPARE MUSSELS

Before cooking, mussels must be carefully scraped and washed to remove barnacles, sand, and the "beard" that attaches them to the rocks or poles on which they grow.

1 △ With a small knife, detach and discard any weed or "beard" from the shells. Discard any mussels that have broken shells or that do not close up when sharply tapped.

2 △ Scrape each mussel to remove any barnacles. Then scrub the mussels thoroughly under cold running water, using a stiff brush. This will remove any harmful deposits from the shell.

61 HOW TO PREPARE SHRIMP

Shrimp have a dark intestinal vein along the back that should always be removed before cooking. The tail shell can be left on, if you like, and removed before eating.

1 △ Peel off the shells from the shrimp with the tips of your fingers. Discard the shells. (The tools made for this task generally do not make the work easier.)

2 △ Using a small knife, make a shallow cut along the back of each peeled shrimp. Then gently pull out the intestinal vein that runs along the back of the shrimp, and discard it.

LIGHT SOUPS

62 MUSHROOM & WILD RICE SOUP
Serves 4–6

Ingredients
1oz (30g) dried mushrooms
½ lb (250g) button
mushrooms
1 celery stick & 1 carrot
1 onion & 1 garlic clove
4–6 juniper berries
4 tbsp butter
½ cup (125ml) port
(optional)
1 bay leaf
6 sprigs fresh thyme
4 cups (1 liter) chicken stock
1 cup (100g) wild rice

1 Prepare dried mushrooms (*Tip 63*).
2 Prepare and slice button mushrooms (*Tip 20*). Reserve a few; roughly chop remainder.
3 Dice celery, carrot, onion; crush garlic and juniper berries. Melt butter in large saucepan; add vegetables and garlic; sauté, 5–7 minutes.
4 Add liquid from soaking mushrooms. Stir in half of the port, chopped mushrooms, bay leaf, juniper berries, thyme sprigs, and chicken stock. Bring to boil, simmer 30 minutes.
5 Bring rice to boil; simmer 30 minutes. Drain.
6 Strain broth into saucepan. Bring to a boil, add reserved and soaked mushrooms, and rice. Simmer 15–20 minutes. Add rest of port; season.

TO SERVE ▷
*Ladle into warmed
soup plates; garnish
with celery leaves.*

REMOVE GRIT
*The liquid from
the soaking
mushrooms
will contain
grit. Line a
sieve with paper
towels and drain
the liquid through
it into a bowl.*

47

△ DRIED MUSHROOMS

63 PREPARE DRIED MUSHROOMS

To prepare dried mushrooms, put them in a bowl, cover with 1½ cups (375ml) warm water, and soak until soft, for about 30 minutes. When you drain off the liquid, rinse the mushrooms in water to remove any grit; drain on paper towels.

64 WHITE MUSHROOM & RICE SOUP

Serves 4–6

Ingredients
1lb (500g) button
   mushrooms
1 celery rib
1 carrot
1 onion & 1 garlic clove
6 sprigs fresh thyme
4 tbsp butter
1 bay leaf
4 cups (1 liter) chicken
   stock
1 cup (100g) long-grain
   white rice
1 cup (250ml) light cream
2 tbsp cut chives

PURÉEING BROTH
Use a blender to purée broth. Depending on how you blend it, you can make the soup any texture from roughly chopped to very smooth.

TO SERVE ▷
Serve in warmed plates, garnished with whole chives. The cut chives in the soup will make a fine contrast.

1 Slice and roughly chop mushrooms (*Tip 20*). Dice celery, carrot, and onion. Crush garlic clove and discard skin.
2 Strip all thyme leaves from sprigs.
3 Make the broth as in Steps 4–5, Tip 62; do not strain.
4 Cook rice in boiling salted water until tender, 10–12 minutes. Drain and set aside.
5 Remove bay leaf from the broth and purée broth until finely chopped but not smooth.
6 Return puréed mushroom soup to pan and stir in drained rice and cream.
7 Heat soup until very hot, but do not boil since it may separate. Remove from heat, stir in cut chives, and season to taste.

65 LIGHT VEGETABLE BROTH

Serves 6–8

Ingredients
1 large leek
2 celery ribs
1 small fennel bulb
3–4 small carrots
2–3 sprigs fresh basil
2–3 sprigs flat-leaf parsley
1lb (500g) tomatoes
6 cups (1.5 liters)
vegetable stock

1 Trim and slice leek (*Tip 22*); trim, peel, and dice celery. Trim stalks and root end of fennel bulb, discarding any tough outer pieces from the bulb; cut bulb lengthwise into quarters and thinly slice.
2 Peel and trim carrots. Cut grooves in side with a small, sharp knife. Slice thinly.
3 Tear basil and chop parsley leaves (*Tip 26*).
4 Peel and coarsely chop tomatoes (*Tip 23*).
5 Bring stock to a boil; add vegetables and simmer until tender, 5–7 minutes.
6 Stir in chopped tomatoes and simmer for 2 minutes more. Remove from heat; season.

TO SERVE ▷
Serve with Parmesan dumplings (Tip 66); sprinkle with torn basil and chopped parsley.

66 PARMESAN DUMPLINGS

Trim and discard crusts from 2 slices of white bread; crumble with your fingers. In a small bowl, beat 1 egg. Combine bread crumbs, 2 tbsp grated Parmesan cheese, and a pinch of mustard powder in another bowl. Season. Stir in enough beaten egg to bind the mixture together. Bring a large saucepan of water to simmer. Drop small balls of dough into water and poach, 1–2 minutes, or until firm.

67 CLEAR BROTH WITH CUCUMBER

For this variation of light vegetable broth, prepare the vegetables and make the soup as in Tip 65. Peel half a small cucumber and cut lengthwise in half. Scoop out the seeds with a teaspoon and cut into thin slices. Add the cucumber to the broth with the tomatoes. Serve hot, with finely chopped basil and parsley and coarsely shredded lettuce leaves.

68 FRENCH ONION SOUP
Serves 6

Ingredients
4 large Spanish onions
4 tbsp butter
6 cups (1.5 liters)
beef stock
2 tsp sugar
1 cup (250ml) red wine
1 small French baguette
1 cup (90g) Gruyère
cheese

TO SERVE △
Serve with cheese-topped croûtes (Tip 91), which absorb the flavor of the soup but remain crisp.

1 △ Peel onions; slice. Melt butter in pan; add onions. Cover onions with circle of waxed paper. Cover; cook 20–30 minutes over low heat. Boil stock to reduce by one third.

2 △ Remove paper from onions and sprinkle with sugar; cook over medium heat until onions are golden brown, 10–15 minutes. Stir well: do not let them darken, or soup will taste bitter.

69 SHALLOT SOUP
Serves 6

Ingredients
1lb (500g) each sweet white or
red onions & shallots
4 tbsp butter & 1 tbsp sugar
6 cups (1.5 liters) chicken stock
4–6 tarragon stalks
1 tbsp Dijon mustard

1 Peel, slice onions and shallots.
2 Melt butter in pan; add onions
and shallots. Cut and butter circle
of waxed paper; place on onions.
Cover; cook 20–30 minutes over
low heat until soft.
3 Remove paper; sprinkle with
sugar. Cook until onions and
shallots are brown, 10–15 minutes.
4 Add chicken stock; bring to boil,
simmer 30 minutes. Chop tarragon;
add with mustard to soup. Stir well.

3 △ Add reduced stock and wine;
partially cover; simmer for 30
minutes. Prepare croûtes with baguette
(*Tip 91*); coarsely grate cheese. Ladle
soup into heatproof bowls. Preheat
broiler to high; set bowls on baking sheet.

TO SERVE ▽
*Serve over croûtes (Tip 91) and garnish
with chopped tarragon leaves.*

4 △ Float 2 croûtes on surface of each
serving; sprinkle with grated cheese.
Slide bowls under broiler, close to the
heat. Broil until cheese is golden brown,
about 2–3 minutes.

70 CHICKEN & MADEIRA CONSOMMÉ

Serves 4–6

Ingredients

6 cups (1.5 liters) chilled
chicken stock
2 celery ribs
2 carrots
2 leeks
1½ lb (750g) plum
tomatoes
¾ lb (375g) chicken wings
and backs
3 egg whites
¼ cup (60ml) Madeira

TO SERVE ▷
Cut up the flesh of the two
remaining tomatoes into
strips and divide evenly
between bowls. Serve with
Melba toast (Tip 94).

1 Gently heat stock in a large pan until very warm. Remove any fat and let cool.
2 Prepare and dice celery, carrots, leeks (*Tip 22*), and all but two tomatoes (*Tip 23*).
3 Remove and discard skin and fat from the chicken. Chop meat into small pieces.
4 In a large bowl, whisk egg whites until frothy. Add vegetables, chicken, and stock. Stir well.
5 Return mixture to pan and bring to a boil; whisk constantly. As soon as liquid is frothy, stop whisking.
6 Clarify (*Tip 11*) and strain liquid.
7 Bring soup almost to a boil, then add Madeira.

71 CHICKEN & ORANGE CONSOMMÉ

Serves 4–6

Ingredients

6 cups (1.5 liters) chilled
chicken stock
2 celery ribs
2 carrots & 2 leeks
¾ lb (375g) chicken wings
and backs
3 large oranges
3 egg whites
¼ cup (60ml) Madeira

1 Follow Steps 1–5 of Tip 70, omitting the tomatoes. Grate zest from two oranges and add with ingredients to egg whites. Stir well.
2 Clarify consommé (*Tip 11*) and strain. Bring back almost to a boil; add Madeira.
3 Using a vegetable peeler, pare zest from 1 orange; cut into fine julienne strips. Add to pot of boiling water; simmer for 2 minutes. Drain.
4 Add julienne to consommé; serve.

COLD SOUPS

72 VICHYSSOISE
Serves 8

Ingredients
1 onion
2 bunches leeks
6 medium potatoes
2 tbsp butter
4 cups (1 liter) chicken stock
2 cups (500ml) milk
1 cup (250ml) light cream
1 cup (250ml) heavy cream
1 medium bunch chives

1 Prepare and dice onion. Slice leeks (*Tip 22*); wash slices well to remove any grit. Peel potatoes and slice thinly; immediately place slices in cold water to prevent any discoloration.

2 Melt butter in a large pan, add onion and leeks, and cook, stirring occasionally, until soft but not brown, 7–10 minutes. Add drained potatoes and stock and bring to a boil. Cover and simmer for 30 minutes, stirring occasionally, or until potatoes are very tender.

3 Purée the soup until smooth. Work the purée through a sieve to remove any leek fibers.

4 Return the soup to the pan and stir in the milk and light cream. Bring the soup just to a simmer, then remove from the heat.

5 Stir in heavy cream and taste for seasoning. Pour soup into a bowl and let cool. Cover; chill thoroughly for at least 3 hours.

6 Finely slice chives. Stir half of chives into soup and season to taste. If soup is too thick, stir in more stock.

◁ **TO SERVE**
Ladle soup into chilled soup plates and garnish each serving with a sprinkling of chopped chives.

53

73 CHILLED FENNEL SOUP
Serves 8–10

Ingredients
1 bunch leeks
1 small onion
6 medium potatoes
2 fennel bulbs
2 tbsp butter
4 cups (1 liter) chicken stock
½ tsp fennel seeds
1 cup (250ml) light cream
2 cups (500ml) milk

TO SERVE ▷
Garnish the well-chilled soup with the feathery tops from the fennel bulbs.

1 Slice leeks (*Tip 22*). Prepare and dice onion (*Tip 16*). Peel potatoes and slice thinly.
2 Trim stalks and roots from fennel. Cut each bulb lengthwise into quarters, then slice thinly.
3 Melt butter in a large pot; add leeks, onion, and fennel. Cook, stirring occasionally, 7–10 minutes. Add potatoes, stock, and fennel seeds. Cover; simmer for 30 minutes; stir occasionally.
4 Purée soup until smooth. Work purée through sieve to remove any leek fibers.
5 Return soup to pot; stir in cream and milk. Bring soup just to a simmer. Pour into bowl; let cool. Cover; chill for at least 3 hours.

74 MINT ICE CUBES
Fresh mint frozen in ice cubes makes a refreshing garnish for chilled soups in hot weather.

You can make the ice cubes up to two days in advance; store them in the freezer until ready to use.

1 △ Boil water and let it cool in the saucepan. Strip mint leaves from their stalks.

2 △ Half-fill each compartment of an ice-cube tray with cooled water. Add leaves; freeze.

3 △ Add more cooled water to the ice-cube tray to fill compartments. Return to freezer.

75 ICED CUCUMBER SOUP
Serves 4–6

Ingredients
2 medium cucumbers
6 scallions
3 sprigs fresh mint
1 cup (250ml) cold chicken stock
1 cup (250ml) plain yogurt
½ cup (125ml) sour cream
Juice of 1 lemon

To Serve ▷
Put three mint ice cubes (Tip 74) in each bowl. Serve with garlic pita toast (Tip 100).

1 Trim ends of cucumber; cut lengthwise in half; scoop out seeds. Cut flesh into strips; dice.
2 Trim and chop scallions.
3 Strip mint leaves from stalks and chop finely.
4 Put cucumber, scallions, and chicken stock in processor; purée until smooth. Add yogurt, sour cream, lemon juice; purée again.
5 Transfer purée to a bowl; stir in mint; season to taste. Cover soup, chill until cold, 1 hour.
6 If too thick, add more stock and lemon juice.

76 CHILLED SPINACH SOUP
Serves 4–6

Ingredients
3 sprigs fresh mint
6 scallions
2 garlic cloves
1lb (500g) spinach
2 tbsp vegetable oil
1 cup (250ml) cold chicken stock
1 cup (250ml) plain yogurt
½ cup (125ml) sour cream
Juice of ½ lemon

To Serve ▷
Serve cold with lemon twist and Melba toast (Tip 94).

1 Strip leaves from mint springs and finely chop.
2 Trim and finely chop scallions. Prepare garlic (*Tip 21*). Discard ribs and stalks from spinach. Wash leaves.
3 Heat oil in frying pan. Sauté scallions, garlic, and spinach, 3–4 minutes. Add chicken stock; bring to a boil. Simmer about 10 minutes.
4 Let cool slightly; purée in a food processor.
5 Transfer to bowl and let cool. Stir in yogurt, sour cream, mint, lemon juice. Season to taste. Cover and chill, at least 3 hours.

77 CHILLED GUACAMOLE SOUP
Serves 6

Ingredients
2 limes
2 large avocados
1 cup (250ml) cold chicken stock
1 cup (250ml) sour cream
1 tbsp tequila (optional)
1 dash Tabasco sauce
2 medium tomatoes
6 sprigs fresh cilantro

TO SERVE ▽
Ladle soup into chilled bowls and garnish. Serve with tortilla chips.

1 Cut limes in half and squeeze juice.
2 Prepare avocados (*Tip 78*); place flesh in large nonmetallic bowl. Add lime juice and stock; purée with hand blender until smooth. Add sour cream, tequila, and Tabasco sauce; purée again briefly to blend. Season to taste; add more lime juice, Tabasco, and extra seasoning if required.
3 Cover soup tightly and refrigerate until well chilled, at least 1 hour.
4 Prepare and dice tomatoes (*Tip 23*); strip leaves from cilantro stalks with your fingers and coarsely chop with a chef's knife.
5 Stir three-quarters of the diced tomatoes and chopped coriander into the soup; reserve the rest for garnish. If the soup seems too thick, add more stock. Taste soup again for seasoning.

TORTILLA CHIPS
To add to the flavor of tortilla chips, grate ½ cup (60g) of Cheddar cheese, and cut and finely dice a red chili. Spread the chips on a baking sheet, scatter the cheese and chili over them, and broil close to the heat until the cheese has melted and is bubbly.

78 HOW TO PREPARE AVOCADOS

To prepare an avocado, you must first remove both the pit and the skin. A ripe avocado will give gently when squeezed. Cut lengthwise around the avocado with a knife.

1 △ Twist the avocado with both hands to loosen the halves; pull the halves apart gently.

2 △ With a sharp tap, embed a knife blade in the pit, and twist it free of the flesh.

3 △ Scoop out the flesh with a spoon. Coat with lemon juice to prevent discoloration.

79 CHILLED AVOCADO SOUP

Serves 6

Ingredients
1½ lemons
3 large avocados
1½ cups (375ml) cold chicken stock
½ cup (125ml) medium-dry white wine
1 cup (250ml) sour cream
1 tsp Worcestershire sauce

1 Squeeze juice from lemons.
2 Prepare avocados (*Tip 78*); reserve one half for garnish. Scoop out remaining flesh and place in large nonmetallic bowl.
3 Add stock and 2 tbsp lemon juice; purée with hand blender until smooth.
4 Add wine, sour cream, and Worcestershire sauce; purée again briefly to blend. Taste for seasoning; add more lemon juice if required.
5 Cover soup tightly and chill for at least 1 hour.
6 Stir soup and add a little more stock if it seems too thick. Season again to taste.

TO SERVE ▷
Serve in chilled soup plates with cheese crackers, and garnish with diced avocado.

80 GAZPACHO
Serves 4–6

Ingredients
2 slices white bread
¾ cup (175ml) tomato juice
4 tbsp red wine
6 medium ripe plum tomatoes
2 garlic cloves
4 scallions
1 red pepper
1 large cucumber
3 tbsp olive oil
2 tbsp red wine vinegar

1 Trim and discard crusts from bread. Break into pieces and place in small bowl.
2 Add tomato juice and red wine; set aside to soak. Prepare and chop tomatoes (*Tip 23*); set aside some for garnish. Prepare garlic (*Tip 21*); trim and slice scallions.
3 Prepare and dice pepper (*Tip 19*); with one half, cut finer dice and reserve for garnish.
4 Peel cucumber, cut lengthwise in half, scrape out seeds; dice. Reserve some dice for garnish.
5 Put bread mixture and prepared vegetables into a food processor and purée until smooth. Transfer to a large bowl; stir in olive oil and vinegar. Cover; chill for at least 1 hour.
6 Stir the soup; taste for seasoning. If it is too thick, stir in a little iced water.

◁ **TO SERVE**
Pour soup into chilled bowls; add 1–2 ice cubes to each if you like. Garnish with reserved pepper and cucumber, and croûtons (Tip 95).

81 GREEN GAZPACHO WITH CRAB

Serves 4–6

Ingredients

2 slices white bread
1 cup (250ml) dry white wine
2 garlic cloves
4 scallions
2 green peppers
1 large cucumber
3 sprigs cilantro
3 sprigs flat-leaf parsley
4 tbsp olive oil
Juice of 1 lime
2 tbsp rice vinegar
8oz (250g) cooked fresh or canned crabmeat

TO SERVE ▷
Ladle into chilled soup plates; add 1–2 ice cubes to each. Garnish with herbs and chopped black olives.

CRABMEAT
Fresh crabmeat can contain bits of broken shell and cartilage, and needs to be properly prepared before eating. Spread the crabmeat on a plate and pick it over with a knife tip to remove any unwanted bits. Then coarsely flake the meat before serving.

1 Trim and discard crusts from bread. Break into pieces and place in small bowl.

2 Add white wine; set aside to soak.

3 Prepare garlic (*Tip 21*). Trim and slice scallions; dice peppers (*Tip 19*). Peel cucumber, cut lengthwise in half, scrape out seeds, and cut into small dice.

4 Strip leaves from cilantro and parsley, reserving 4–6 tiny sprigs for garnish.

5 Put all ingredients into a food processor and purée until smooth. Transfer puréed mixture to a large bowl and stir in olive oil, lime juice, and vinegar. Cover; chill for at least 1 hour.

6 Stir soup. Taste for seasoning and add more lime juice, vinegar, and seasoning if required.

7 Prepare crabmeat and add to each serving.

82 HUNGARIAN SOUR CHERRY SOUP
Serves 4–6

Ingredients
1lb (500g) sour cherries
½ cup (100g) sugar
3 cups (750ml) medium-
dry white wine
Juice of 2 lemons
2 tbsp Kirsch
3 cups (750ml) crème
fraîche or light sour cream

TO SERVE ▷
*Garnish with crème
fraîche and sprinkle
with a little cinnamon.*

1 Discard cherry
stalks; remove pits,
using the tip of a
vegetable peeler.
2 Put cherries into saucepan. Add sugar and
wine. Heat, stirring occasionally, until sugar has
dissolved. Bring to a boil; cover, simmer until
cherries are soft, 5–7 minutes. Cool slightly.
3 Pour cherry mixture into blender or food
processor. Purée until smooth. Work purée
through sieve. Stir in lemon juice.
4 Stir in Kirsch and three-quarters crème fraîche
until evenly mixed. Cover; chill for 2 hours.

83 MAKING CRÈME FRAÎCHE
To make crème fraîche, use
2 cups (500ml) heavy cream and
1 cup (250ml) buttermilk. Make
sure the buttermilk specifies "live
cultures" on the label. Chill the
crème fraîche before serving.

1 ◁ Pour heavy cream
into saucepan; add
buttermilk. Stir to mix.
Heat until cream feels
just warm (75°F/24°C).

2 ▷ Pour mixture into
bowl; cover, leaving a
gap for air. Stand at room
temperature until cream
has thickened, 6–8 hours.

SHORT CUTS

84 PLAN AHEAD

Most soups can be prepared a few days ahead. Some soups, such as gumbo, improve when kept a day or two because their flavors mellow and blend. Only soups with perishable or lightly cooked ingredients must be made before serving.

CHICKEN & HAM GUMBO ▷

85 REHEATING SOUPS

Many soups, such as spiced carrot and orange, require reheating after the ingredients have been puréed. At this stage, taste the soup for seasoning, adding more salt and pepper if required. If the soup is too thick, add more of the basic stock to thin the mixture.

◁ SPICED CARROT & ORANGE SOUP

86 FREEZING SOUPS

Make a full or double batch of your favorite soup and freeze it in quantities to serve two, four, or six people. Don't forget to label each container for identification. Fill containers only two-thirds full so the liquid can expand during freezing, and will not boil over if reheated in the microwave.

87 MICROWAVE

The microwave can be put to good use when making soups. Use it to speed up preparations such as heating stock if you are short of time, or to defrost stock you have prepared earlier. When heating soup in the microwave, be sure to stir it before serving so that no "hot spots" remain.

PRESENTATION

88 CHOOSING BOWLS

The enjoyment of a soup has much to do with its visual impact. Puréed soups are best served in traditional soup bowls and plates, while clear soups look nice in plain bowls. Cold soups are attractive served in shallow soup plates.

An earthenware bowl is best for a hearty soup

TO SERVE
The ingredients of a soup can determine which bowl to use.

89 GARNISHES FOR SOUPS

A sprinkling of toasted nuts, herbs, or citrus zest, a pattern of a contrasting sauce, or just a little cluster of vegetable julienne; all make effective garnishes. Any garnish should contrast with the appearance of the soup, and highlight its texture and flavor.

△ **CHILLED SPINACH SOUP**
Add a twist of lemon to each serving to contrast with the deep green of the liquid.

△ **GOLDEN PEPPER SOUP WITH PESTO**
Cilantro or basil pesto can be used to create interesting patterns on a soup.

90 CREAM DECORATIONS FOR SOUPS

Patterns made with heavy cream are an attractive finishing touch for puréed soups. Three simple designs are shown below, but you can experiment with many others. All you need is about 4 tbsp of heavy cream, a knife, and some imagination.

CIRCLE OF HEARTS ▷
From the tip of a teaspoon, slowly drip heavy cream onto the surface of each plate of soup to form a circle of drops. Then carefully draw the tip of a small knife through the drops to create a perfect circle of hearts around the edge of the soup.

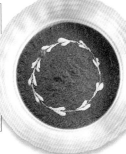
△ CIRCLE OF HEARTS

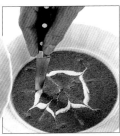
△ FIVE-PETAL FLOWER

◁ FIVE-PETAL FLOWER
Using a teaspoon, slowly drizzle a circle of cream onto the surface of each plate of soup. Then feather the circle by drawing the tip of a knife through the cream first in one direction, then the other. You will quickly create an impressive flower.

JAUNTY PINWHEEL ▷
Place about 1 tbsp of heavy cream onto the surface of each plate of soup. Draw the tip of a small knife away from the center to make an even pattern of curved spokes. You can make stars and other patterns in the same quick and simple way.

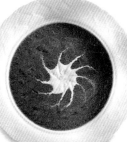
△ JAUNTY PINWHEEL

63

91 HOW TO MAKE CROÛTES

Crisp and crunchy croûtes are ideal to serve with French onion and many other soups. They are simple to make: All you need is a small French baguette or long French roll, and some butter.

1 ▷ Preheat the oven to 350°F/180°C. Slice baguette diagonally into ½in (1.25cm) slices, discarding the ends. Melt 2 tbsp butter. Lightly brush both sides of each slice with the butter. This helps them brown.

2 △ Place bread slices on baking sheet and bake in oven until they are dry and lightly browned, turning them over once, 7–12 minutes.

92 SUN-DRIED TOMATO CROÛTES

Spreading croûtes with a butter and sun-dried tomato purée adds a zesty finishing touch to this traditional accompaniment to soups. Use tomatoes packed in oil; pat dry on paper towels before cutting up. Experiment with other toppings, such as grated cheese.

1 ◁ Cut 2 sun-dried tomatoes into small pieces and purée with 4 tbsp butter. Season with pepper. Cut baguette into diagonal slices.

2 ▷ Lightly toast on one side. Turn over, spread with purée, and toast again.

93 CORNBREAD STICKS
Makes 14

FRESHLY BAKED

Ingredients
4 tbsp butter
1¼ cups (150g) yellow cornmeal
1 cup (125g) all-purpose flour
1 tbsp sugar
1 tsp salt
1 tbsp baking powder
1 cup (250ml) milk
2 eggs

1 Preheat oven to 425°F/220°C.
2 Melt the butter. Sift cornmeal, flour, sugar, salt, and baking powder into a bowl; make well in center.
3 Whisk milk and eggs until combined. Pour them into well. Add melted butter to well. Mix gently with a wooden spoon until combined.
4 Pour mixture into a buttered corn-stick mold or into buttered 8in (20cm) square cake pan. Bake until a skewer inserted into center comes out clean, about 20–25 minutes.
5 Let cool slightly, remove from mold or pan, and cool on wire rack. If you are using a cake pan, cut cornbread into squares.

Mixture should come just to top of molds

◁ **TRADITIONAL TREAT**
Use a corn-stick mold to make these traditional cornbreads.

94 MELBA TOAST
Preheat oven to 325°F/170°C. Toast 6 medium slices of white bread on a baking sheet until light brown, 7–9 minutes. Cut off the crusts. Place your palm on each slice and split bread horizontally, cutting between toasted surfaces. Cut wafer-thin slices into triangles; lay toasted side down on baking sheet and bake until crisp, about 10 minutes.

CRISPLY TOASTED

95 HOW TO MAKE CROÛTONS

Croûtons are an appealing and crunchy garnish for puréed and creamed soups. Fry the bread cubes in vegetable or olive oil for crispness, or in 4 tbsp butter if you prefer the flavor.

 △ Trim the crusts from 3 slices of bread. Cut into small cubes. Heat 4 tbsp oil in a frying pan, add cubes; fry until brown, 2–3 minutes.

2 △ Remove pan from the heat. Lift out croûtons with a slotted spoon and drain well on paper towels. Toss croûtons with finely chopped parsley.

96 FRIED SPICED CROÛTONS

For this spicy version of croûtons, combine 1 tsp curry powder and 1 large pinch each of ground cardamom and nutmeg in a bowl. Add freshly ground black pepper to taste.

1 △ Trim the crusts from 3 slices of bread. Cut into small cubes, and fry in 4 tbsp oil until brown on all sides. Combine the spices in a bowl.

2 △ Sprinkle spice mixture over the croûtons, stir to mix, then take pan off heat. Lift out croûtons with a slotted spoon and drain well on paper towels.

97 OVEN-TOASTED CROÛTONS

To make oven-toasted croûtons, brush three slices of bread with a little oil and toast them in a preheated oven at 375°F/190°C until they are browned on both sides.

1 △ Stamp out shapes with a small cutter, or cut into cubes.

2 △ Place on a baking sheet; toast in oven, turn once, 5–12 minutes.

△ TO SERVE
Serve as garnish on puréed and creamed soups.

98 SESAME-SEED TWISTS

Makes 24

Ingredients
8oz (250g) prepared puff pastry
1 egg & ½ tsp salt
1½ tbsp sesame seeds

1 Preheat oven to 425°F/220°C.
2 Sprinkle baking sheet with water. On a lightly floured surface, roll out puff pastry dough to a rectangle approximately 8 x 12in (20 x 30cm).
3 Lightly beat egg with salt. Brush pastry dough with egg glaze. Sprinkle sesame seeds evenly over dough; press them down lightly.
4 Cut dough into 24 strips ½in (1.25cm) wide. Lift each strip and twist it along its length a few times. Lay on baking sheet and press each end down firmly; chill 15 minutes.
5 Bake until crisp and golden brown, 10 minutes.
6 Transfer to wire rack and let cool.

99 PARMESAN CRACKERS
Makes 12

Ingredients
¾ cup (100g) all-purpose flour
Large pinch of cayenne
5 tbsp (75g) butter
1 cup (90g) freshly grated
Parmesan cheese
¼ cup (30g) walnut pieces
1 egg & ½ tsp salt

Gently knead dough until pliable

1 ◁ Sift flour, cayenne, and seasoning into a bowl. Cut in butter; add cheese. Mix well; press dough together. Knead dough, 2 minutes. Wrap tightly; chill, 30 minutes.

2 △ Coarsely chop walnuts. Roll out dough to a 5 x 7½in (12.5 x 19cm) rectangle, about ⅜in (1cm) thick. Cut into triangles.

3 △ Preheat oven to 375°F/190°C. Place triangles on baking sheet. Beat egg and salt, glaze wafers, sprinkle with walnuts. Chill 15 minutes.

4 △ Bake in preheated oven until wafers are golden brown, 15–18 minutes. Let cool 4–5 minutes, then transfer to wire rack to cool fully.

100 GARLIC PITA TOASTS
Peel and finely chop 2 garlic cloves. Combine with 3 tbsp olive oil in a bowl. Cut three oval pita breads crosswise in half, then into quarters, on the diagonal. Trim; discard all long rounded edges from triangles. Open up and separate triangles. Brush inside each piece with garlic and olive oil mix; place, oiled side up, on baking sheet. Bake at 425°F/220°C until lightly brown, 8–10 minutes.

OPENING PITA BREADS

101 PIROSHKI
Makes 25–30

Ingredients
1½ cups (175g) all-purpose flour
1 egg & 1 tsp salt
2 tbsp sour cream
4 tbsp unsalted butter
½ carrot & 1 onion
½ cup (60g) green cabbage
½ cup (60g) farmer cheese
2 tsp caraway seeds
1 egg beaten with ½ tsp salt

PIROSHKI

1 △ Sift flour onto work surface. Make well in center; add egg, salt, sour cream, and butter in pieces. Mix ingredients together until smooth. Chill 30 minutes; roll out ⅛ in (3mm) thick.

2 △ Chop carrot, dice onion; sauté in pan until soft, 3–5 minutes. Let cool. Chop cabbage and soak in boiling water for 2 minutes; drain and cool. Mix well with carrot, onion, farmer cheese, and caraway; season. Cut out rounds from dough with cookie cutter; place mixture on half of each round.

3 ◁ Brush edge of each round with egg and salt glaze. Pinch edges of dough together to seal. Transfer to baking sheet; brush with glaze. Chill 15 minutes. Preheat oven to 400°F/200°C. Bake until brown, 15–18 minutes.

INDEX

ACKNOWLEDGMENTS

DK would like to thank Hilary Bird for compiling the index,
Fiona Wild for proofreading, Pat Alburey for editorial assistance,
and Robert Campbell for DTP assistance.

Photography
All photography by David Murray and Jules Selmes,
assisted by Ian Boddy and Steve Head.